O Hijab Esvoaçante

The Swirling Hijaab

Na'ima bint Robert
Nilesh Mistry

O hijab da minha mãe é preto,
amplo e macio,

My mum's hijaab is black and soft
and wide,

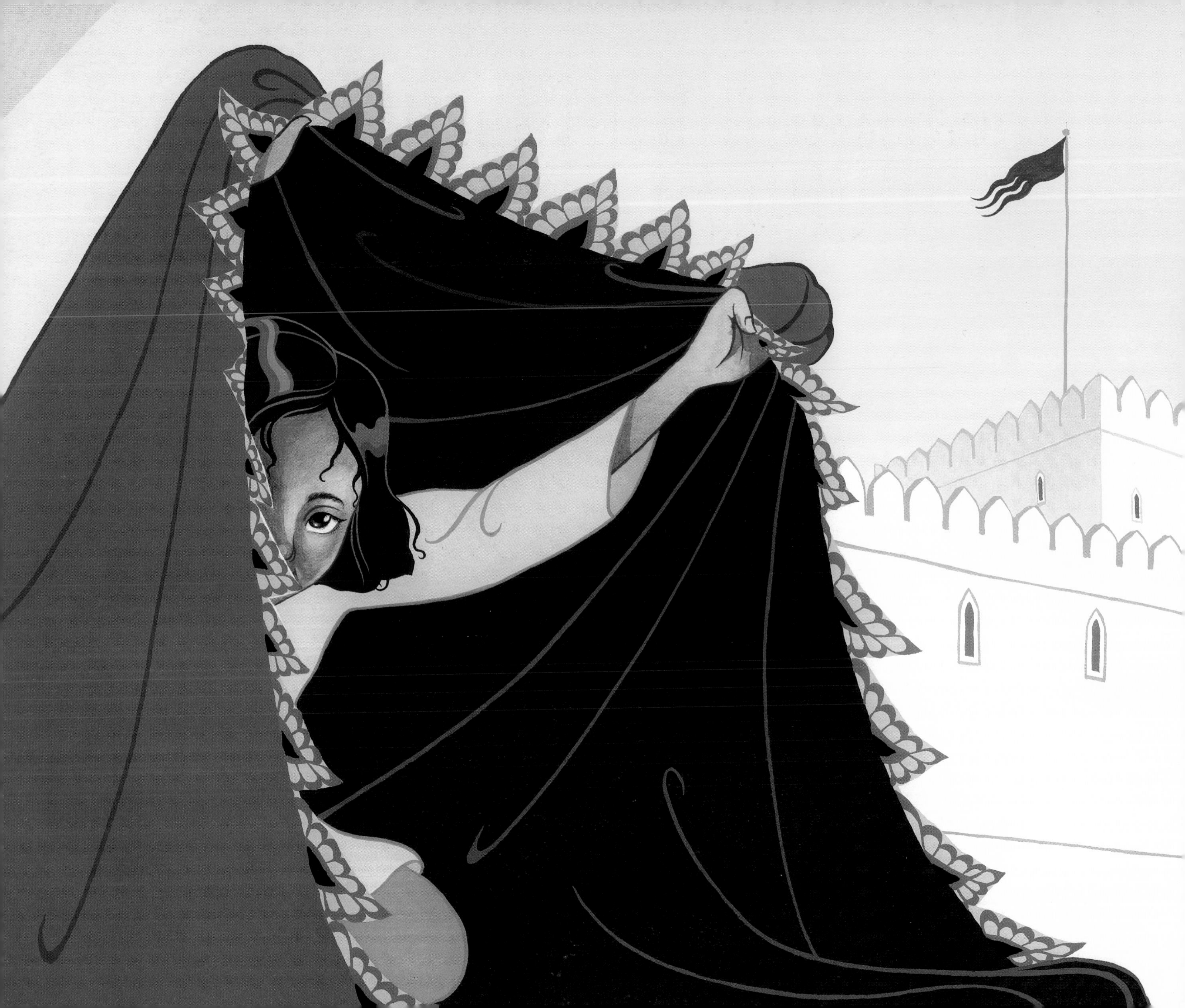

Uma fortaleza onde me posso esconder!

A fort for me to hide inside!

As velas agitadas de um barco,
batendo ao vento,

A ship's sails flapping in the air,

Um consolo quando ela não está.

A comforter when she's not there.

Uma tenda de beduíno,

A bedouin tent,

Um sari de casamento,

A wedding sari,

Uma toalha de mesa para um lanche especial.

A cloth for my tea party.

A capa de uma rainha guerreira,

A warrior queen's cloak,

A bagagem de um nómada,

A nomad's baggage,

Uma mantinha quando preciso
de descansar!

A blanket when I need a rest!

Mas o hijab serve mesmo é para
cobrir a minha mãe,
como parte da sua fé.

But covering my mum
as part of her faith
Is what the hijaab does best.

Bismillahir-Rahmanir-Raheem

For the daughters of Islam, past, present and future

N.B.R.

For Saarah, Farheen & Rayaan

N.M.

The Swirling Hijaab is one of many sound enabled books.
Touch the circle with TalkingPEN for a list of the other titles.

First published in 2002 Mantra Lingua Ltd
Global House, 303 Ballards Lane, London N12 8NP
www.mantralingua.com

A CIP record for this book is available from the British Library